MW01054063

Sofer

The Story of a Torah Scroll

Rabbi Dr. Eric Ray
with Joel Lurie Grishaver
& Jane Golub

Torah Aura Productions

I wish to dedicate this book to my fellow Scribes of all Ages, to the Rabbis and Tzadikim who were my teachers and to my beloved family. Also to my good friends Reb Shmuel Zadock, "Sofer s'tam", who helped me become a Torah Scribe and Rabbi Mordecai Waxman who commissioned me to restore and rewrite my first complete Sefer Torah. — Dr. Eric Ray

היום לפני/ וזל השבעות / זמן מתן תורתנו/ תשל"ו

For us the development of **Sofer** was an act of love. For a long time, Eric has been both a friend and a teacher. He is even warmer and more special in person. We would like to thank Debi Mahrer Rowe for her refelections upon the original manuscript and Carolyn Moore Mooso for copyediting the book in its first edition. We would like to thank Susan Haubenstock for copyediting the second edition of Sofer. — The Torah Aura Production Team

Library of Congress Cataloging-in-Publication Data

Ray, Eric

Sofer; the story of a Torah scroll

Summary: A Jewish scribe explains in detail how he shapes the Hebrew letters he uses in transcribing the Torah and how he prepares the scrolls themselves.

1. Torah scrolls—Juvenile literature. 2. Scribes, Jewish—Handbooks, manuals, etc.—Juvenile literature. 3. Calligraphy, Hebrew—Juvenile literature. [1. Torah scrolls, 2. Scribes, Jewish—Handbooks, manuals, etc. 3. Calligraphy, Hebrew.] 1. Grishaver, Joel Lurie. II. Title.

BM657.T6R39 1986	296.6'1	85-58480
0-933873-98-0	(pbk.)	

Copyright © 1999 Eric Ray

Published by Torah Aura Productions • 4th Printing

All rights reserved. No part of this publication may be reproduced or transmitted in any form or by any means graphic, electronic or mechanical, including photocopying, recording or by any information storage and retrieval system, without permission in writing from the publisher.

TORAH AURA PRODUCTIONS• 4423 FRUITLAND AVENUE, LOS ANGELES, CA 90058
(800) BE-TORAH • (800) 238-6724 • (323) 585-7312 • FAX (323) 585-0327
E-MAIL <MISRAD@TORAHAURA.COM> • VISIT THE TORAH AURA WEBSITE AT WWW.TORAHAURA.COM

MANUFACTURED IN THE UNITED STATES OF AMERICA

My name is Eric Ray. I am a Jewish artist and teacher. In the past I have made many paintings and designed ads for magazines. I have used my skills as an artist to forge fake papers, which helped Jews get out of Holocaust camps and go to Palestine before it became Israel. I also worked on some of the State of Israel's first maps. Now I create Jewish art for synagogues and for people's homes. I think the most important part of my art is being a *sofer.*

סוֹבֵר *Sofer* is the Hebrew word for a scribe. A scribe is someone who writes down important books and texts in beautiful, clear handwriting. Being a sofer is an important Jewish job that artists have done for thousands of years.

3

I am a סוֹפֵר סת״ם Sofer S'TaM. S'TaM is a word made out of the first letters of the three most important things a sofer writes.

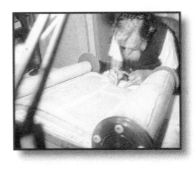

ס

S=*Sefer Torah*. The Torah is made up of the five books of Moses and is the book that is the life of the Jewish people. The Sefer Torah, from which we read in synagogue, is a scroll that must be handwritten by a *sofer.* The *Sefer Torah* is made up of long rolls of handwritten parchment that have been sewn together and rolled on wooden rollers.

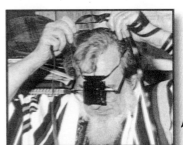

ת

T=*Tefillin*. In the Torah God tells the Jewish people, "Take to heart these words which I command you today." God also says, "Bind them as a sign on your hand and let them serve as a symbol on your forehead." To help Jews obey this mitzvah, the *sofer* writes down four parts of the Torah, including the Shema. The *sofer* then puts these words in leather boxes called tefillin, which you can bind to your hand and hang as a symbol on your forehead.

ם

M=*Mezuzah*. In the Shema God also says: "write them on the doorposts of your house." To help Jews obey this mitzvah, the *sofer* writes down part of the Shema and places it in a container called a mezuzah, which can be nailed to the doorpost of a Jewish home.

I do most of my work in my studio, which is in the attic. When you visit me you will find all kinds of tools and supplies lying all over. Artists use all kinds of things to help with their work. Because I am a *sofer*, you'll also find Hebrew words and letters in almost every corner. I really love both words and letters.

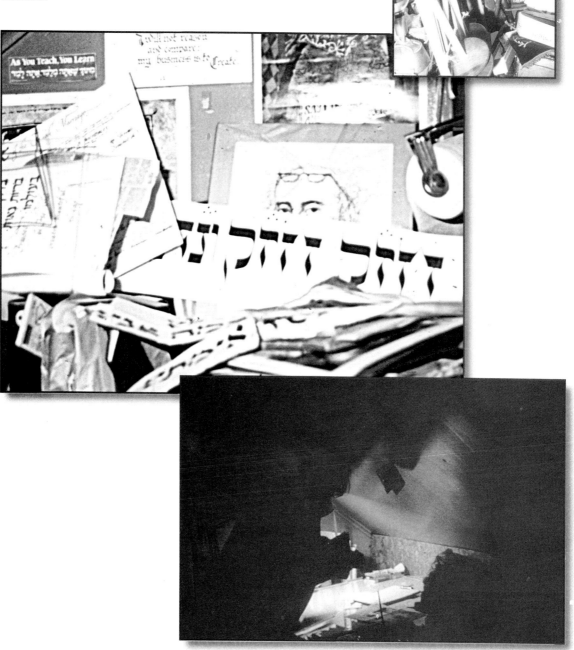

There are thousands of ways to shape and design Hebrew letters. In the Talmud, a book of Jewish law, we are told that a *Sefer Torah*, *Mezuzah*, or *Tefillin* can be written only in square letters called K'tav Ashuri. This alphabet was written in these letters.

Alef is the first letter in the Hebrew Alef-Bet. The *Alef* looks like it is standing on one foot and reaching its hand up to God' The *Alef* always looks like it is moving; like it is always going somewhere. It is a letter that dances.

Alef

Bet, on the other hand, rests solidly on the ground. *Bet* is a house with an open side, a floor, a back wall, and a roof. *Bet* is always open to the future, always open to the next letter or the next word we write in Hebrew.

Bet

Gimmel was originally the picture-letter for a camel. When I write a *Gimmel* I can see a camel bending down with its front knees folded. Some people look at a *Gimmel* and see a man walking and kicking one leg forward. Letters are wonderful; people can make them into lots of things.

Gimmel

A Dalet is written by drawing two lines. The first goes across the top, and the second goes down. When you draw this second line you twist your pen and make a foot. I always see the Dalet as a letter that is running forward. I think the Dalet is running to catch up with the Hey. Hey is the letter that is used twice in God's most important name.

Dalet

Hey

Hey is the most holy letter. It is shaped like a sukkah—the little booth that we decorate with leaves and fruit during the holiday of Sukkot. Every Jewish family built and lived in a sukkah during the forty years of wandering in the wilderness. Just like the letter Hey, the sukkah taught Jews that God's love is always with us.

Vav is the sixth letter in the Hebrew Alef-Bet. Vav reminds us of the six days of creation leading up to Shabbat. To me the Vav looks like a shofar standing on the mouthpiece. I write a Vav and think about Rosh ha-Shanah and how the great shofar will sound when the Messiah comes.

Vav

Zayin means a weapon, and it looks something like a battle-axe. It is also a special letter because its head is bent. Almost every other letter has a flat top. I like to think of the Zayin as looking like a Jew standing in prayer.

Zayin

Het is a letter made up of two other letters.
There are two different ways of writing a Het. One
sofer will write it as a Vav and a Zayin that are
connected with a little roof. Another sofer will write it
as two Zayins. Can you tell which one I used here?

Het

The Tet looks like it is pointing to itself. Tet begins the
word טוֹב tov, which means "good." Every time I see a
Tet it teaches me that a Jew has to look into his or her
heart, as we do on Yom Kippur, and try to be a good
person. This is the most important lesson in the Torah.

Tet

The Yud is from יָד yad, which means hand. When you look at it you can
see a hand. It also sounds like Yid, which in Yiddish means a Jew.
What is more, the Yud is the first letter in God's most important name.
Yud is a letter that flies up off the ground. Sometimes I think the Yud is
God's outstretched hand reaching down to every Jew. Yad, Yud, and Yid
are all connected.

Yud

Kaf can make two sounds. It can sound like a "K." Or
it can make the sound of clearing you throat that comes
at the end of the word בָּרוּךְ barukh. Barukh, which
means "bless," is a word we use in many of our prayers.
Kaf looks like an open mouth. You always have to open
your mouth to say a blessing.

Kaf

I think the *Lamed* is special. Every time I write a *Lamed* I see it as an arm and a human hand pointing a finger up to God. The *Lamed* reminds people that we are here only because God created us. I think *Lamed* is one of the most beautiful of letters.

Lamed

Mem is the letter that begins both Moses' and his sister Miriam's names. *Sofrim*, scribes, have a tradition that when you are writing a *Sefer Torah*, you always use five pen strokes to write a *Mem*. The five pen strokes are for the five books of Moses—the Torah.

Mem

There is an ancient tradition that the *Nun* looks like a snake, but I don't see it that way. In the *Sefer Torah* you write the *Nun* with a head resting on a body that looks like it is sitting. Then a *sofer* puts a three-stroke crown on top. This reminds us that every Jew can earn the crown of Torah.

Nun

Samekh sounds like the Hebrew word שָׂמֵחַ *same'ah*, which means "happy." *Samekh* is a round letter. Every time I write a *Samekh* I want to add two dots and a mouth and turn it into a happy face.

Samekh

9

The Ayin is supposed to be an eye. If you look closely you can almost see a triangle. Look on the back of a dollar bill and you'll also see an eye in a triangle. It is the ancient symbol for the mystical "inner eye" or for the "all-seeing" eye of God.

Ayin

Peh looks like a face. You can see the nose, the mouth, and maybe the point of a beard. Sometimes I think I can see Moses' face in the Peh.

Tzadi

Peh

The Kuf is a galloping letter. To me it looks like an ostrich running across the desert. The Kuf also looks like it is carrying a bundle over its shoulder. I think that being a Jew means galloping forward with the bundle of our history over our shoulder.

Tzadi is the letter of righteousness. Its name even sounds like צדיק tzadik, a righteous person. When you look at it you can see both of its hands reaching out and giving help.

Kuf

10

Resh is my letter, because it is the letter that begins my last name, "Ray." My father was a hairdresser. When he worked on his customers he bent over them like a *Resh*. When I sit and work over the Torah I think that I am bending like a *Resh*.

Resh

Shin is the first letter in one of God's names, *Shaddai*. This is the name on the front of the mezuzah. *Shin* has three strokes at the top. *Shin* reminds me of the first three Jewish fathers: Abraham, Isaac, and Jacob. I also remember the three partners in making a Jewish family: the mother, the father, and God. For me, it is the *Shin* in שׁדי *Shaddai* (in the mezuzah hanging on the door) that really turns any house into a Jewish home.

Shin

Tav is the final letter in the *Alef-Bet*. When one writes a *Tav* it ends with a walking foot. Just like the *Alef, Tav* is always moving forward. It seems to teach you that you never really get to the end.

Tav

This is just like the holiday of *Simhat Torah*, when Jews read the last words in the Torah and then go right back to the beginning and read the first words again. Every end is a new beginning.

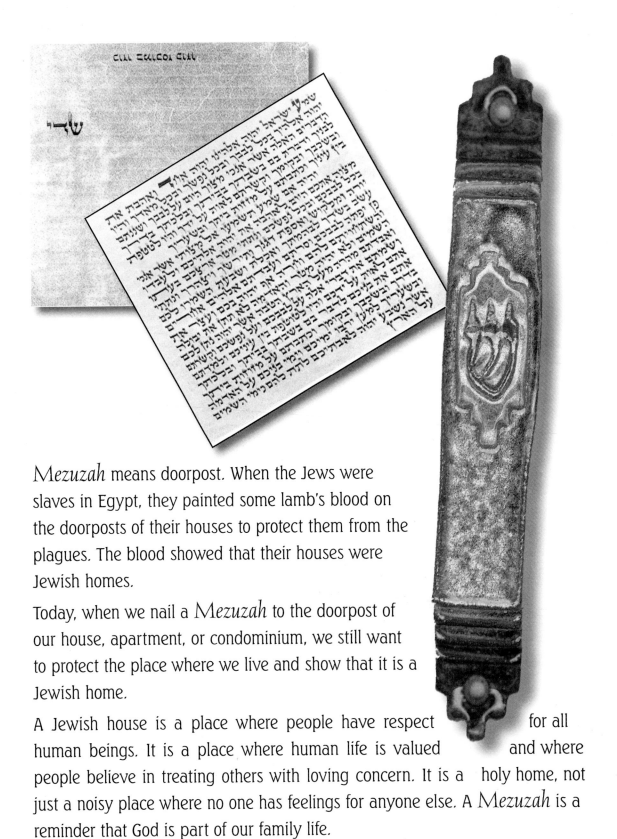

Mezuzah means doorpost. When the Jews were slaves in Egypt, they painted some lamb's blood on the doorposts of their houses to protect them from the plagues. The blood showed that their houses were Jewish homes.

Today, when we nail a *Mezuzah* to the doorpost of our house, apartment, or condominium, we still want to protect the place where we live and show that it is a Jewish home.

A Jewish house is a place where people have respect for all human beings. It is a place where human life is valued and where people believe in treating others with loving concern. It is a holy home, not just a noisy place where no one has feelings for anyone else. A *Mezuzah* is a reminder that God is part of our family life.

On the front of the *Mezuzah* is the word שַׁדַּי Shaddai, which is one of God's names, "The Almighty." Shaddai also stands for the three beginning letters of the Hebrew words:

שׁוֹמֵר דְּלָתוֹת יִשְׂרָאֵל

Shomer Delatot Yisrael

God guards the doors of Israel

Putting up a *Mezuzah* is a way of asking God to protect our house, and a way of reminding ourselves to make our house a Jewish home.

Writing a *Mezuzah* is a lot more than just copying words.

The *Tefillin* are like the *Mezuzah*. Both are commanded in the same paragraph in the Torah and both contain handwritten portions of the Torah. Both the *Mezuzah* and the *Tefillin* are reminders to a Jew to let the words of the Torah guide his or her life.

The *Tefillin* are really two leather boxes containing scrolls with parts of the Torah written on them. During weekday morning prayers these boxes are fastened to the arm and to the head by leather straps.

One box is called the שֶׁל רֹאשׁ *Shel Rosh*, and it is hung "as a symbol" on the forehead. It reminds us that our thoughts and intelligence should always by used to do God's work. This box is made of four sections joined together. It reminds us of the four mothers of Israel: Sarah, Rebecca, Rachel, and Leah. God's love, like our mothers' love, is always with us.

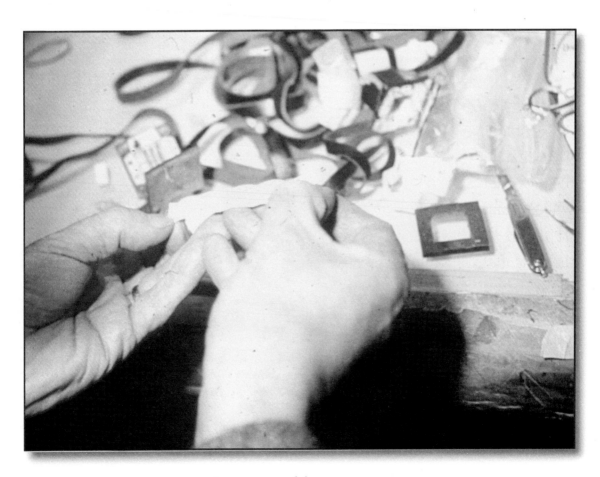

The other box is called the שֶׁל יָד *Shel Yad*, and it is "bound" to the arm near the heart. It reminds us that all of our feelings and all of our strength should be used to make the world a better place.

When a *sofer* makes a pair of *Tefillin* there is a lot more to the job than just carefully hand-lettering the Hebrew. The *sofer* must shape the boxes out of the hide of a kosher animal, mold the two letter *shins* onto the של יד *Shel Yad*, cut the straps out of leather and tie their knots in exactly the right way, then sew everything together. Finally, all of the leather must be dyed black.

It takes a lot of work to make a pair of *Tefillin*. But it is not only the craft of the *sofer* that is important. While making a pair of *Tefillin* a *sofer* must direct his thoughts to the importance of his work. Jews believe that the spirit of the *sofer* is important and that the feelings and thoughts a *sofer* has while working on the *Tefillin* make a difference.

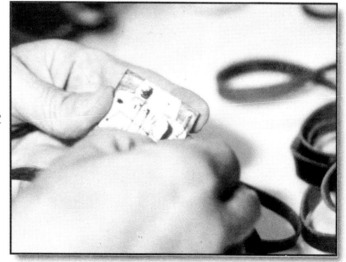

Writing a *Mezuzah* or the parchments for the pair of *Tefillin* or a *Sefer Torah* is holy work. There are all kinds of rules a *sofer* must follow. These come from the Talmud and other books of Jewish law.

The first rule is that no "base metals" may be used in making or repairing these texts. Base metals are the metals used in everyday tools. That means that no iron, no steel, no brass, no copper, and no bronze can be used. Base metals are the kinds used to make weapons. Nothing that is used for killing can be used in making a *Sefer Torah*, a *Mezuzah*, or a pair of *Tefillin*. It is okay to use tools made of silver or gold,

or ivory or fine woods. The same rule about "base metals" applies to the *yad*, the pointer we use for marking our place when we read Torah, so it, too, is made out of silver or gold, or ivory or fine wood.

The pen used to write these texts cannot be made of metal either. The first *sofrim* used pens made from reeds like papyrus. They cut them and shaped them into pens. Later *sofrim* began using quills. A quill comes from the longest feather in a bird's wing tip. A *sofer* has to cut the quill and shape the pen point just perfectly. Today almost every *sofer* writes with a quill made from a turkey feather.

KOSHER INK RECIPE

For writing *Sifre Torah, Tefillin* and *Mezuzot.*

Boil one pint of water.

Add ½ pint of (crushed) gallnut powder.

Add ¼ pint of (crushed) gum arabic crystals.

Add 1/8 pint of (crushed) copper sulfate crystals.

Add 1/8 pint of (crushed) fine black carbon powder.

Making the ink a *sofer* uses is like cooking. The basic recipe is found in the Talmud, but every *sofer* has his own tricks for making his own ink.

Gallnuts are made when a gall wasp stings a tree. Just as people do, the tree swells from the sting. The wasp will lay her eggs in the gallnut,

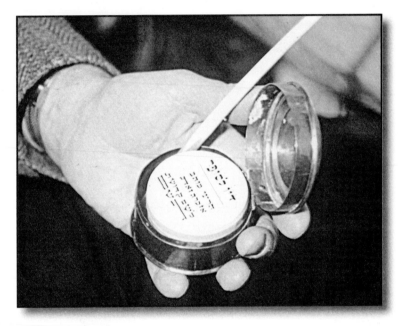

which is the perfect food for the baby wasps. This perfect food also makes the ink used to write a Torah.

Gum arabic is a kind of glue made from the sticky sap of special plants. This is the part of the formula that sticks the letters to the parchment.

Copper sulfate is a blue crystal that turns the gallnut liquid black as it gets older and as it is exposed to air. This is what makes the ink stay black forever.

Black carbon is just ground up charcoal or soot. In the beginning the gallnut ink is grey and not very dark. The black carbon makes it black so the *sofer* can see what he is writing.

I know how to make "kosher ink," but I am not a great "ink" cook. When I need ink I go and buy it. I go to Williamsburg, the part of Brooklyn where lots of Hasidim live. I visit my friend Rabbi Saul Arye Zoldan, who is also a *sofer.* I buy my ink from him. He is a wonderful ink "chef" and a master scribe.

The ink comes packaged in baby bottles. Whenever I buy a bottle of ink I smile. I think that the baby bottle is the perfect package. The words I write with that ink feed and nourish the Jewish people.

The Torah is not written on paper. It is written on kosher animal skins called vellum or parchment. We call a piece of parchment a *k'laf*. It takes a lot of work to prepare a *k'laf*, and there are many rules to follow.

No animal may be killed just for its skin. Only if an animal was killed for food or died of natural causes can we use its hide to make parchment. First the animal's hide is softened by soaking it in clear water for a number of days. Then, to remove all the hairs, the skin is soaked in lime water for eighteen days. A lot of scraping has to be done to remove all the fat and hairs. After all this soaking the *k'laf* comes out all wrinkled and bundled together. Look in the picture and you can see a piece of treated *k'laf*. To make the *k'laf* into a smooth writing surface it must be dried on a stretching rack. When you work on a *Sefer Torah*, or on a *Mezuzah* or on *Tefillin*, your feelings are very important. The person who makes the animal hide into *k'laf* must say out loud that this *k'laf* is being prepared especially to make a *Sefer Torah*.

When I visit my friend Rabbi Zoldan I also buy my *k'laf* from him. He has boxes of rolled parchments all over his studio.

To be a *sofer s'tam* a person must be of good character. A *sofer s'tam* must be a person who lives a fully Jewish life.

The work of writing a *Sefer Torah* begins early in the morning when the *minyan* gathers. It is a Jewish custom to pray with a *minyan* (a group of at least ten Jews) three times a day. I begin my work every day by praying with the *minyan* at my congregation and by always putting some money in the *tzedakah* box.

When I come home from services I am ready to work. The first thing I do is wash my hands. It is a Jewish custom to wash hands before every holy act.

We don't wash our hands just to make them clean. It isn't like a doctor preparing to do surgery. We wash our hands to prepare our mind and heart to do something holy.

The next thing a *sofer* does seems funny at first. I take out a scrap of kosher *k'laf* and write the name of Israel's ancient enemy. I write the name: *Amalek.* עֲמָלֵק

And then I cross it out. עֲמָלֵק

When the people of Israel had just escaped from Egypt they had to do a lot of walking in the wilderness. Moses put the soldiers in the front of the group to protect the people. In the back of the long line were the mothers with their young children, as well as the older people who couldn't walk as fast. *Amalek* was a cruel people who attacked Israel from the back, killing and hurting those who could least defend themselves. They were evil. God commanded us to "blot out the memory of *Amalek.*"

So a *sofer* begins every day of work by blotting out the memory of *Amalek.* It is a way of saying that the Torah is a model of how to do good and not evil.

22

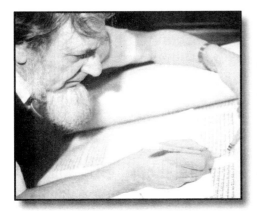

Then I am ready for work. When I take a fresh piece of *k'laf* I need to make it ready. First I need to rule the lines, which will keep my letters straight and even. I use a *sargel*, which is a tool for scratching lines into the parchment. My *sargel* is made out of a thorn. Remember that no base metals can be used on the Torah.

When you are a sofer you work with a top line. I begin the top of every letter on the line I have scratched. There is no bottom line. Each line on the *k'laf* marks the top of a new line.

Writing the Torah is slow, careful work. It takes about three years to write a whole Torah. Before he writes even a single word, the *sofer* must first say a *brakhah*, a blessing. Writing a Torah is a *mitzvah*, a holy action.

A *sofer* isn't allowed to write even one word of the Torah from memory. Every word and every letter must be checked. We use a book called a *tikkun*, which has a perfect text, to make sure that no mistakes are made.

When I write I do what every *sofer* does; I sing every word and every letter out loud. When you visit my studio you'll hear me working:

Yisrael

Yud,

Sin,

Resh,

Alef

and

Lamed sofit.

Saying *"sofit"* reminds me that this is the last letter of the word. Before and after every word I have to check my work in the *tikkun*.

Each sheet of parchment used in the Torah is called a *yeriah*. On it you will find between three and eight columns of writing. It takes about 250 of these sections to make up a full *Sefer Torah*. A *Sefer Torah* is really very long. If it were rolled out, it would be longer than a football field. Each *yeriah* must be checked by three rabbis before it can be used.

A *sofer* works on only one *yeriah* at a time. Each section is written and checked before it is sewn into the Torah.

It takes a lot of love and dedication to write a Torah.

Most people think that a *sofer* is not allowed to make a mistake, but they are wrong. When you write a Torah you are allowed to correct any mistake made in any word except for God's name.

When I have to erase a mistake I do it by scraping the letters off the parchment. I use a special tool I have made from pieces of glass. Can you figure our why I use glass and not a razor blade?

I spend a lot of my time repairing and rewriting old Torah scrolls. Jewish law is very detailed on what it takes to make a Torah kosher. Kosher really means "okay for Jews to use". In the Torah every letter must be clear and readable. No part of it can be blurred or smudged. No two letters can be touching. Even if a letter is cracked because the parchment split a little bit, the Torah cannot be used.

Even though Jews are very careful and treat a Torah scroll with great respect, using a Torah wears out the writing. Synagogues send me their old Torah scrolls, and I go through them word by word and letter by letter. I make sure that every single letter in the Torah is beautiful and perfect.

A Hasidic rabbi named Uri of Strelisk said, "The Torah is like the Jewish people. If one single letter is left out of a Torah, then it is unfit for use. If one single Jew not part of the Jewish people, then they are incomplete. If two letters in the Torah are touching, then the Torah is unfit for use. If every Jew does not have his or her own special relationship with God, then the Jewish people are incomplete."

I like to think that every time I fix a Torah I am also helping to make the Jewish people a little stronger.

Writing God's name is the most important part of writing a Torah. When a *sofer* writes God's name there are lots of special preparations.

On a day when I am going to write God's name I go to the *mikveh*. A *mikveh*

Please Pay up your yearly Dues

General Dues ____ °°

Men that use Mikveh '35°°

See Mrs. Dreyfus or Send to

Cong. Mikveh Israel *They are Tax Deductable*

71-11 Vleigh Pl. *Flushing N.Y.* 11367

is a special pool of natural running water that a Jew uses to make himself or herself pure. For Jews, going to the *mikveh* helps us direct our hearts and our minds. It is like washing your hands and saying a *brakhah*.

28

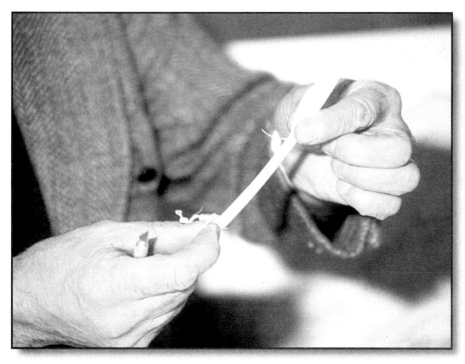

To write God's name I use a special quill that has never been used to write any other words. I mark my *Ha Shem* quills by leaving part of the feathers on one side. I remove all the feathers from my regular quills.

To write God's name I use a special bottle of ink, which is used only to write God's name. No pens except my Ha-Shem quills have ever touched it.

Every day I say a *brakhah* before I start writing the Torah. When I write God's name I must say another *brakhah*.

For Jews, their relationship with God is very important. Torah is the gift that God gave the Jewish people. In writing the Torah, and especially in writing God's name, we show lots of respect.

Let me tell you one trick that I do, that lots of *sofrim* do. When it is difficult to get to the *mikveh* every day, I save up all the times I have to write God's name. I write everything else on a page, but not God's name. Then once or twice a week I go to the *mikveh*, take out my special tools, and spend the day writing in God's name. It is easier to work that way, and it is easier to really direct my heart toward each writing of God's name.

The last part of the work is sewing *yeriah* to *yeriah* and attaching them to the two wooden rollers, which are called *atzei ḥayyim*, the trees of life. We Jews call the Torah a tree of life.

For the sewing I use a silver needle and a silver thimble, both of which are gold-plated. I also have a pair of gold-plated scissors, which I use for cutting things. For thread I use what we call *gid*. This is a part of the sinew from the leg of a kosher animal that has been twisted into a thread. We may not use any thread other than kosher *giddin*.

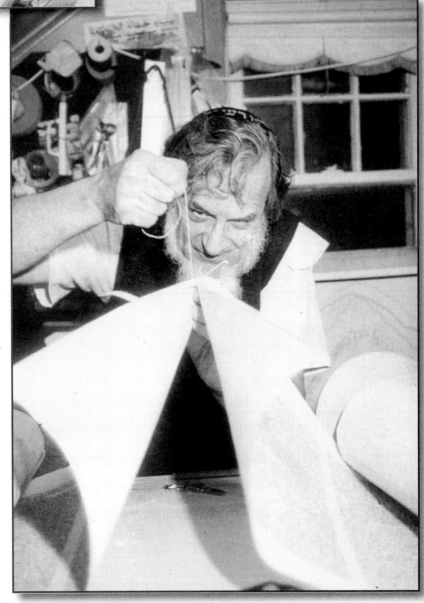

We Jews are a funny people. We like to connect things to certain special moments in our past and tie them all together.

We remember that Jacob's name was changed to Israel, which means a "man of God." He changed his name because he changed the kind of person he was in order to become one of the fathers of the Jewish people. He wrestled with an angel and in that struggle he conquered all the childish things in his past. During that struggle the angel twisted his thigh so that it would always remind him to behave like a "man of God." From that time on we have used twisted tendons from an animal thigh to sew together the pieces of the Torah. The *giddin* remind us that we must always try to be better, even when it is a struggle.

Being a *sofer* is very special. For more than 3,000 years Jewish artists have struggled with quills, inks, and parchments. They have used their skills to keep the chain of Torah alive.

The Torah is the book that holds the wisdom of the Jewish people. It is our history. It is the story of the journey of the Jewish people toward a better world. It is the record of the laws and values by which we live.

The writing of the *Sefer Torah* must be done by a dedicated Jew who loves the Torah. No machine can do the work I do, because a *Sefer Torah* can be made only by human hands.

I really love being a *sofer s'tam.*